GREAT SPORTING EVENTS

Cricket

Clive Gifford

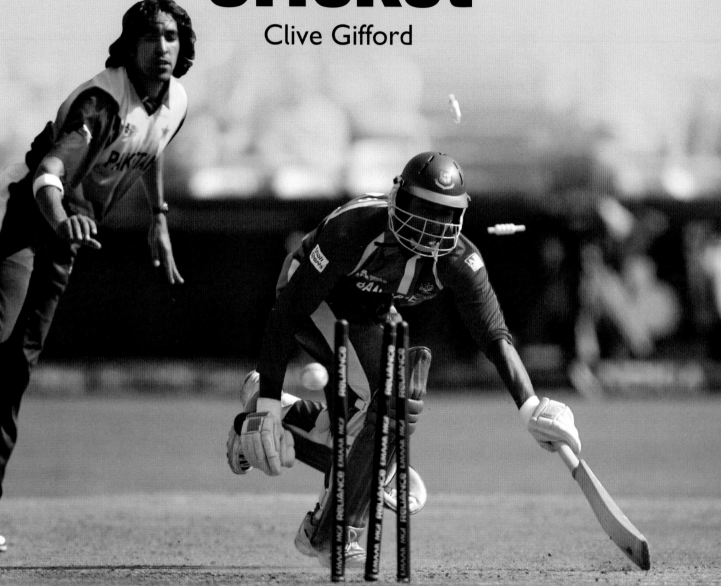

W
FRANKLIN WATTS
LONDON • SYDNEY

First published in 2011 by Franklin Watts
338 Euston Road, London NW1 3BH

Franklin Watts Australia
Level 17/207 Kent Street, Sydney NSW 2000

Editors: Katie Dicker and Gerard Cheshire
Art Direction: Rahul Dhiman (Q2AMedia)
Designer: Cheena Yadav and Ravinder Kumar
(Q2AMedia)
Picture Researcher: Debabrata Sen (Q2AMedia)

Picture credits:
t=top b=bottom c=centre l=left r=right

Front Cover: Aijaz Rahi/AP Photo.
Back Cover: Ross Setford/AP Photo, Aijaz Rahi/
AP Photo, Dave Thompson/AP Photo, Mark J.
Terrill/AP Photo, Jay LaPrete/AP Photo, Anja
Niedringhaus/AP Photo.
Title Page: Carl Fourie/AP Photo.
Imprint Page: Lee Smith/LV Championship.
Insides: Karel Prinsloo/AP Photo: 4, Themba
Hadebe/AP Photo: 5, Sandra Mu/Getty Images:
6, Ajit Solanki/AP Photo: 7, Lee Smith/LV
Championship: 8, Richard Heathcote/Getty Images:
9, Darren England/Newspix/Rex Features: 10,
Tertius Pickard/Gallo Images/Getty Images: 11,
Bikas Das/AP Photo: 12, Obed Zilwa/AP Photo: 13,
Ross Setford/AP Photo: 14l, Corey Davis, Pool/AP
Photo: 14r, Rick Rycroft/AP Photo: 15, Aijaz Rahi/
AP Photo: 16, Carl Fourie/AP Photo: 17, Aman
Sharma/AP Photo: 18, Aman Sharma/AP Photo: 19,
Tom Hevezi/AP Photo: 20, Jon Super/AP Photo: 21,
Rob Griffith/AP Photo: 22, Tom Hevezi/AP Photo:
23, Jack Dawes/Daily Mail/Rex Features: 24, AP
Photo: 25, Quinn Rooney/Getty Images: 26, Alastair
Grant/AP Photo: 27, AP Photo: 28.

A CIP catalogue record for this book
is available from the British Library.

ISBN: 978 1 4451 0190 3

Dewey Classification: 796.3'58

Note: At the time of going to press, the statistics
in this book were up to date. However, due to the
nature of sport, it is possible that some of these may
now be out of date.

Printed in China

Franklin Watts is a division of Hachette Children's
Books, an Hachette UK company.
www.hachette.co.uk

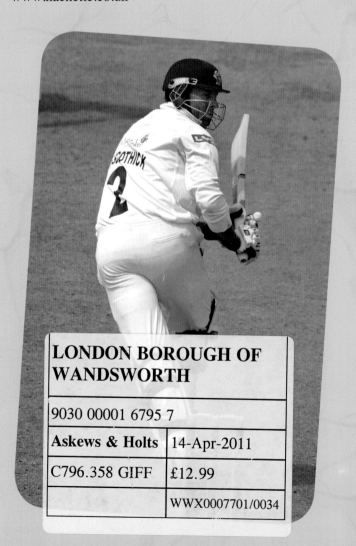

Contents

*Words in **bold** are in the glossary on page 30

Batting and bowling

Cricket is a bat-and-ball sport with 11 players in each team. One team bats with two players at a time, each trying to score **runs**. The other team fields and bowls the ball, with six bowls making up each **over**. The fielding team tries to get the opposing batsmen called 'out', and also tries to stop them from scoring runs. The team that scores the most runs wins.

They're out!

Each batsman plays until he is called out (also known as losing their **wicket**). This can occur in a number of ways, including being bowled (when the ball bowled by the bowler hits the **stumps**), caught (when a fielder catches the ball hit by the batsman before it hits the ground) or run out (when a fielder throws the ball to hit the stumps whilst the batsman is out of his **batting crease**). Once out, a player is replaced by another batsman from their team. When ten players are out, the team's **innings** is over. In **limited overs** games (see page 12) a team also finishes their innings once they have faced their set number of overs.

Pakistan batsman Kamran Akmal prepares to play a shot as he stands in front of his stumps.

Reaching the boundary

The edge of a cricket ground is called the **boundary** and is usually marked by a rope. A strike of the ball that reaches the boundary scores four runs (a 'four') if it bounces on the ground beforehand, or six runs (a 'six') if it passes the boundary still airborne.

Fit and focused

Although cricket can be seen as slow-paced compared to some sports, it is not a gentle game. Top players have to be fit and focused. When batting, they wear plenty of protective clothing as the fastest bowlers can bowl at speeds approaching 140kph (90mph). The **wicket-keeper**, who fields the ball behind the stumps, is often protected with leg pads, body padding and a helmet.

In competition

World cricket is organised by the International Cricket Council (ICC). Many different competitions exist for men's cricket, women's cricket and youth team cricket all over the world.

GREAT SPORTING STATS

Catches often win matches and a team's wicket-keeper is in the best position to take a catch behind the batsman. South African wicket-keeper Mark Boucher has taken 478 catches in Test matches, a record.

Record-breaking South African wicket-keeper Mark Boucher is well protected from the fiercest of deliveries.

First-class cricket

First-class cricket is the highest level of cricket played by clubs, regions or other teams in a country. First-class cricket matches are usually held over three or four days of action and feature two batting innings for each side.

National competitions

Every major cricketing nation has a first-class competition, from the County Championship in Britain (see pages 8–9) to the Quaid-i-Azam Trophy in Pakistan. In the West Indies, the regional four-day competition has sometimes invited an overseas team, such as England A or the Kenyan national cricket team, to take part.

Plunket Shield

New Zealand's first-class championship is one of the longest-running cricket competitions. It was first held in 1906. It has been known by many names, but is currently called the Plunket Shield and runs from November to April. The four-day games are intense and long. There are more than 120 overs and over six hours play each day. Of the six competing teams, only the Otago Volts have not won the competition in the past six seasons.

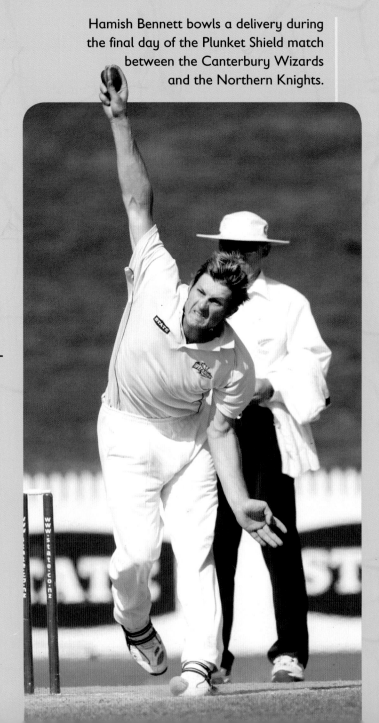

Hamish Bennett bowls a delivery during the final day of the Plunket Shield match between the Canterbury Wizards and the Northern Knights.

The Ranji Trophy

The Cricket Championship of India, now known as the Ranji Trophy, began in 1934. It features a two-tier system, with the Super League at the top and a 12-team Plate League below. The best teams from the Plate League join the Super League teams for a mixture of **round robin** games, followed by a knockout competition. The 2009/10 winners, Mumbai, are also the competition's most successful side with a staggering 39 trophies.

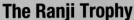

GREAT SPORTING STATS

The three highest individual batting scores of all time have been in first-class competitions in England, Pakistan and Australia. These are: 501 not out – Brian Lara playing for Warwickshire v Durham, 1994. 499 – Hanif Mohammad playing for Karachi v Bahawalpur, 1959. 452 not out – Donald Bradman playing for New South Wales v Queensland, 1930.

Vikram Solanki, playing for Rajasthan in the Ranji Trophy, strikes the ball while the Gujarat wicket-keeper looks on.

The County Championship

The County Championship, held in England and Wales, is the longest-running first-class competition in the world. It was first held in 1890, with eight sides representing English counties. It now includes 18 county teams, including one based in Wales (Glamorgan) and its newest recruit, Durham, which joined in 1992.

Marcus Trescothick, playing for Somerset, hits a four during a County Championship game.

Busy season

The County Championship season starts in April and ends in September. All teams play a hectic schedule of 16 four-day matches, fitted in between other competitions. Most teams feature at least one overseas player. In 2009, Pakistan's Danish Kaneria took the most County Championship wickets (75) of all bowlers while playing for Essex.

County grounds

Each county team has one or more home grounds where they play eight matches. Some, such as Lords (used by Middlesex), Edgbaston (Warwickshire) or Old Trafford (Lancashire) are also famous venues internationally. Some grounds have a reputation for having particularly good conditions for batting or bowling. In 2007, Somerset's county ground, at Taunton, saw two of the top seven highest scores of all time, including 850 runs for seven batsmen (850–7) **declared** by the home team.

21st century changes

In 2000, the County Championship teams were divided into two divisions of nine teams each. At the end of each season, one team is **relegated** and another is **promoted** between the divisions, adding extra tension in matches. No county is safe. In 2007, Sussex won the County Championship, but was relegated from the top division just two years later.

Points scoring

Sixteen points are awarded for a win and three points for a draw. In addition, there are bonus points for good batting or bowling. Durham won back-to-back championships in 2008 and 2009, the latter by a comfortable 54 points. In contrast, Nottinghamshire and Somerset topped the table, both with 214 points, in 2010. Nottinghamshire were crowned champions as they had won more games overall.

GREAT SPORTING
STATS

Bonus points are gained in the first 110 overs of a team's first innings. The 2010 bonus points were:

Batting
200-249 runs = 1 point
250-299 runs = 2 points
300-349 runs _ 3 points
350-399 runs = 4 points

Bowling
3-5 wickets: 1 point
6-8 wickets: 2 points
9-10 wickets: 3 points

Nottinghamshire celebrate winning the County Championship in 2010 after they took a third Lancashire wicket and gained the crucial bonus point to make them champions.

The Sheffield Shield and SuperSport Series

Both South Africa and Australia have similar competitions to the UK's County Championship. The Sheffield Shield, in Australia, and the SuperSport Series, in South Africa, are both held over four days, with each team playing two innings.

The Sheffield Shield

The Sheffield Shield (known as the Pura Cup between 1999 and 2009) is Australia's leading first-class cricket competition. The six states of Queensland, Tasmania, New South Wales, Victoria, South Australia and Western Australia play each other twice over the season. The top two sides face each other in a final match held at the home ground of the team that currently leads the league.

Shane Watson bowls during a Sheffield Shield match between the Queensland Bulls and the South Australia Redbacks.

The SuperSport Series

South Africa's leading competition began in 1889 with just two teams – Kimberley and Transvaal. For almost a century, it was known as the Currie Cup before becoming the Castle Cup and, in 1995, the SuperSport Series. Since 2005, the competition has featured six regional teams playing each other home and away in a ten-match season.

Playing for points

In the SuperSport Series, ten points go to a team for winning a match. Teams batting in their first innings score a bonus point when they reach 150 runs, with a further 0.02 bonus points added for every run above that. This means that should a team make 300 runs in their first innings, they would receive a total of four bonus points. In the 2009/10 **series** the Nashua Cape Cobras won more games than their closest rivals, the Nashua Titans, to win the competition.

GREAT SPORTING STATS

The three leading runs-scorers in the history of the SuperSport competition are Graeme Pollock (12,409 runs), Peter Kirsten (11,835 runs) and Jimmy Cook (11,307 runs). In October 2009, Jimmy Cook's son, Stephen, scored a competition record of 390 runs in an innings, which included 53 fours.

JP Duminy plays an attractive attacking shot for his team, the Nashua Cape Cobras, against the Highveld Lions.

One-day internationals

One-day internationals (**ODIs**) are limited overs matches between two national teams. There have been over 3,000 ODIs since the very first match was played in 1971 as a way of pleasing spectators after rain had washed out an Australia v England Test match (see pages 20–21). ODIs usually offer a definite result in just a single day's play.

Limited overs games

Limited overs games see each team bat for a set amount of overs, provided they still have batsmen in the game. Limited overs competitions within countries (for clubs or counties) are usually 40 overs per side. One-day internationals are now always 50 overs per side.

Sachin Tendulkar is the all-time leading scorer in one-day international games, with over 17,500 runs.

Bowling and fielding

The bowling team looks to stifle runs and get the opposition team out. Each bowler is allowed to bowl a maximum of ten overs. Most ODI sides contain a number of **all-rounders** who can bowl some overs, but are also good batsmen. Every run is crucial, so fielders need to be athletic to dive and stop shots wherever possible.

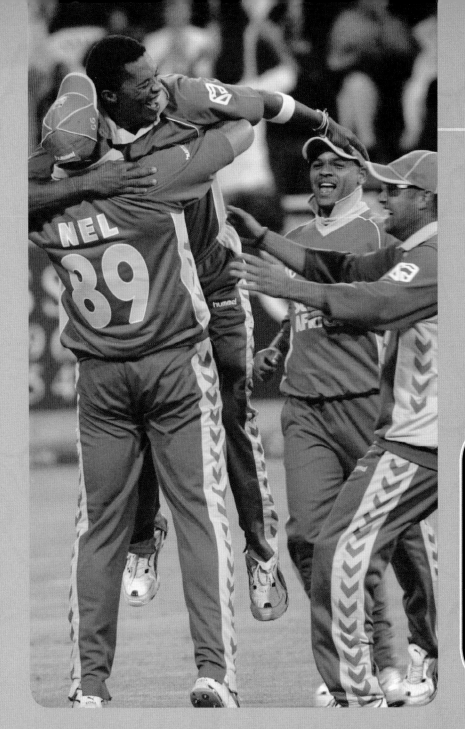

South Africa's Makhaya Ntini is congratulated by teammates after taking a wicket during an ODI match against Australia. He ended with match-winning figures of six wickets for just 22 runs.

GREAT SPORTING STATS

In 2006, there were three mammoth scoring feats in ODIs. Australia racked up 434 runs in an ODI against South Africa, only to find themselves beaten as South Africa reached 438. Amazingly, three months later that score was beaten by Sri Lanka scoring 443-9 against the Netherlands — an all-time record in ODIs.

Powerplays

For 20 of the 50 overs, the bowling team have to operate under what is called a powerplay. This sees them forced to place many fielders close to the batsmen, leaving large parts of the pitch free for potential run-scoring shots. Powerplay gives the batting team a temporary advantage, and adds extra excitement to a match.

ODI series and competitions

ODIs are often scheduled as part of a touring team's matches, meaning that a series of ODIs is normally played before or after a Test match series. Sometimes, a third team is invited to create a triangular tournament. In addition, there are ODI competitions such as the Cricket World Cup (see pages 14–15) and the ICC Champions Trophy, which is held every two years.

The Cricket World Cup

The ultimate ODI competition began in 1975, when England hosted a one-day international tournament of eight teams that was won by the West Indies. The ICC Cricket World Cup, as the competition is now known, is now held once every four years and attracts major attention. For example, the 2007 tournament, in the West Indies, was televised in over 180 countries.

The ICC Cricket World Cup trophy

Pakistan captain, Imran Khan, celebrates as he takes the last English wicket to win the 1992 Cricket World Cup.

World Cup format

All ten of the leading cricket nations (those that have been granted Test match status; see pages 20-21) usually receive an invitation to the tournament. A further four places, or more, are available to teams that perform well in the ICC World Cup qualifying tournament. For the 2011 World Cup, the qualifying tournament took place in 2009 and saw Canada, the Netherlands and Ireland qualify. All of the countries that play take part in a series of group games, which lead to **quarter finals**, **semi finals** and then a final.

Shock results

Recent tournaments have seen some exciting shock results, such as Kenya beating one of the favourite teams, Sri Lanka, in the 2003 World Cup to reach the semi-finals. In 2007, Ireland beat a strong Pakistan side by bowling them out for just 132 runs, whilst Bangladesh surprisingly beat India in the group stage by bowling them all out for 191.

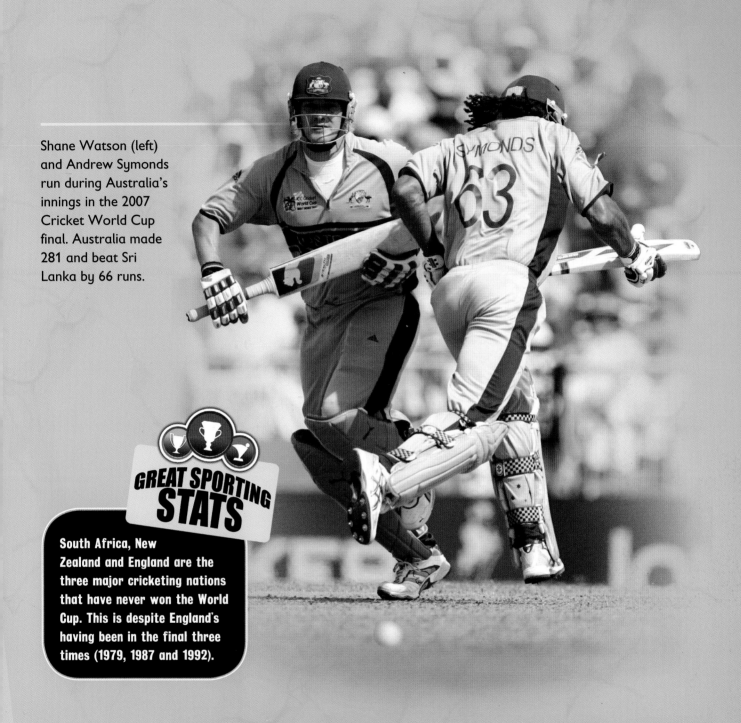

Shane Watson (left) and Andrew Symonds run during Australia's innings in the 2007 Cricket World Cup final. Australia made 281 and beat Sri Lanka by 66 runs.

Best batting

Held in the West Indies, the 2007 World Cup saw a feast of exciting batting. Australia's Adam Gilchrist scored 149 runs in the final against Sri Lanka, whilst South Africa's Herschelle Gibbs struck six sixes off a single over for the first time in World Cup history. Yet the player voted man of the tournament was bowler Glenn McGrath, who took 26 wickets, helping Australia to win their third World Cup in a row.

The Twenty20 World Cup

An exciting new form of cricket began in 2003 and has since boomed in popularity. **Twenty20** cricket is a short, explosive, limited overs contest, with each team batting for just 20 overs. Within four years it had its own World Cup competition, featuring all the world's leading cricket nations.

Twenty20 tournaments

The first Twenty20 World Cup was held in South Africa in 2007, with the second following in England in 2009 and the third in the West Indies in 2010. Each tournament features 12 teams – all the Test match-playing nations, plus two qualifiers, which in the past have included Scotland, Ireland, Kenya and the Netherlands.

England cricketer Craig Kieswetter hits a powerful shot during the final of the 2010 Twenty20 World Cup between England and Australia.

Batting feats

Explosive batting and getting a high **run-rate** are crucial to success. Sri Lanka produced the tournament's highest score, with 260 from 120 balls, against Kenya in 2007. Three Sri Lankans are also in the top six run scorers of the competition. The list is headed by Tillakaratne Dilshan who scored 317 runs in the 2009 tournament.

Super Eights onwards

Divided into four groups of three teams, the teams play two matches to whittle the 12 sides down to the Super Eight stage. Here, the teams are split into two groups of four teams, which play each other. The top two sides from each group play semi-finals to produce the finalists.

Bowling prowess

Although Twenty20 matches are all about runs, a brilliant bowling or fielding performance can also turn a game. Pakistan won the 2009 Twenty20 World Cup mostly due to Umar Gul's astonishing bowling performances that included taking five wickets for just six runs in the match against New Zealand.

GREAT SPORTING STATS

Australia's Matthew Hayden played in only the first Twenty20 World Cup in 2007, but his impact was enormous. He averaged 88.33 runs each time he batted — an incredible feat. The highest individual score at the Twenty20 World Cup was by Chris Gayle, captain of the West Indies side. He scored a staggering 117 runs from just 57 balls against South Africa in 2007.

Bangladesh's Mahmudullah is run out by Pakistan's Umar Gul in the 2007 Twenty20 World Cup. Gul took 13 wickets in the tournament — more than any other bowler.

The Indian Premier League

Founded in 2007, the Indian Premier League (IPL) is a Twenty20 competition held in India during the spring. With thrilling cricket and showbusiness glamour, the tournament attracts a large television audience that enjoys watching Indian stars play with some of the finest overseas players in the game.

Tournament teams

When the IPL was formed, individuals and business groups bid for the right to own one of the eight founding teams (expanded to ten in 2011). Each squad plays all the other sides, both home and away. Two points are awarded for a win and one for a no-result. At the end of the season, the top four teams take part in semi finals before the grand final.

Players for sale

Unique to the IPL is its auction system, with the different teams bidding to buy the world's best players. In the IPL's first season, Indian captain Mahendra Singh Dhoni was the most expensive player at US$1.5 million (£1.04 million), a figure topped by the US$1.55 million (£1.07 million) paid for Andrew Flintoff and Kevin Pietersen in 2009.

Mahendra Singh Dhoni strikes a powerful shot against the Royal Challengers Bangalore. In 2010, Dhoni captained the Chennai Super Kings to win the IPL.

Overseas players

Australia's Shane Warne captained the Rajasthan Royals to victory over the Chennai Super Kings in a thrilling IPL final in 2008, with the winning runs coming with just one ball to spare. Another Royals player from Australia, Shane Watson, was named Man of the Series. The following season it was the turn of Australia's Adam Gilchrist to be voted the IPL's best player as he captained the Deccan Chargers team that beat the Royal Challengers Bangalore in the 2009 final. In 2010, the Chennai Super Kings were champions, beating the Mumbai Indians in the final.

GREAT SPORTING STATS

Scoring is fast and furious in an IPL game, with scores of between 140–170 runs typical from just 20 overs. Yet in one 2008 IPL game, New Zealand's Brendon McCullum of the Kolkata Knight Riders hit an astonishing 158 runs from just 73 balls.

Shane Warne celebrates with other members of his Rajasthan Royals team during an IPL game against the Mumbai Indians.

Test match cricket

Test matches are the longest matches in the sport and are held between the top national cricket teams in the world. These five-day games offer the toughest possible challenge of a player's nerve and skill. They also test a team's ability to handle pressure and tough conditions to win matches.

England's Jonathan Trott bats during a 2010 Test series versus Pakistan. Trott won England's Man of the Series award for his strong batting.

Test history

The first ever Test match took place in 1877, with Australia beating England by 45 runs. Since that time, almost 2,000 Test matches have been played between the ten Test-playing nations, with Bangladesh becoming the latest Test team in 2000. Women's Test cricket began in 1934 and now also includes ten teams, with the Netherlands joining in 2007.

Five-day matches

A Test series consists of between two and six Test matches played in one country. Each Test match involves each team batting for two innings per side over five days' play, with usually about six hours of action each day. Every 80 overs, the fielding team is offered a new ball which is harder and bouncier than the old one.

Building an innings

Patience, stamina, nerve and skill are required to bat long, bowl hard and field skilfully throughout an entire Test match. Teams try to build big innings scores with their batsmen forming partnerships. If a side is struggling, they look to their last batsmen, known as **tailenders**, to stay in for a more established batsman at the other end to continue scoring runs, as well as scoring runs themselves.

Saving a game

Test matches can ebb and flow, with one team and then the other dominating. Bad weather can halt play and stop a team on top from achieving a win. As some matches near their end, a team may try to keep their wickets, so they are still batting at the end of the game. Even if a team has fewer runs, if they are still batting the game will end in a draw rather than a loss. This is called saving the game. In their 2009/10 tour of South Africa, England achieved this twice in four Test matches.

GREAT SPORTING STATS

If a team think they have scored enough runs in their innings and want to move the game on, they can declare the innings whilst they still have wickets left. This was the case in the largest ever Test score. In 1997, Sri Lanka had scored 952 for six wickets. They declared against India to win the game. In 2008, England declared their second innings at 311 for nine against India. A **century** score from Sachin Tendulkar, however, saw India go on to win the Test match!

Shafiul Islam (second left) is surrounded by his Bangladesh teammates after taking the wicket of England's Jonathan Trott during a Test match.

The Ashes

The oldest Test series of all is the epic contest between Australia and England, known as **the Ashes**. The competition gets its name from a tiny urn said to hold the remains of the **bails** burned to celebrate Australia's defeat of England in 1882.

Series details

The Ashes series takes place every two years, but with Australian and English summers occurring at different times of the year, there is either 1½ years or 2½ years between each series. The contest is usually held over five matches, although four-match, and six-match series have been held.

Australian players and fans celebrate in Adelaide, Australia, after Australia won the second Test match of the 2006 series.

Test venues

Some of the most famous grounds in world cricket are used for Ashes series, such as the Melbourne Cricket Ground (MCG), the traditional home of Tests starting on Boxing Day. In England, Lords in London is usually the host of the first match of the series although, in 2009, the teams played the first Test match at Sophia Gardens in Cardiff, Wales.

Changing fortunes

Both teams have had periods of success and dominance but between 1989 and 2005, Australia retained the Ashes in every series. The 2005 Ashes was one of the most dramatic in history, going right to the very last day of the series before England ran out narrow winners at the Oval in London. England were thrashed 5-0 in Australia in 2006/07, but won the series 2-1 in 2009. This leaves the overall tally of 31 Ashes series to Australia, 28 to England and five drawn.

England's Andrew Flintoff celebrates after running out Australian captain Ricky Ponting in the fifth Ashes Test in 2009.

GREAT SPORTING STATS

The most wickets taken by one bowler in an Ashes match is an incredible 19 out of 20 balls by English spin bowler, Jim Laker in the 1956 Old Trafford Test. Overall, Australia's Shane Warne has taken the most wickets in Ashes matches (195) followed by fellow Australians Dennis Lillee (167), Glenn McGrath (157) and England's Ian Botham (148).

The five batsmen who have scored the most runs in Ashes Test matches are:
Donald Bradman (Australia) 5,028
Jack Hobbs (England) 3,636
Allan Border (Australia) 3,548
David Gower (England) 3,269
Steve Waugh (Australia) 3,200

Great players and teams

Test cricket presents an intense challenge of a player's skills. Some players who are chosen by a country's **selectors** fail to perform and are dropped. Others, though, prosper and have long Test cricket careers.

Fearsome and fast

Test cricket has seen a number of great, fiery, fast bowlers who bowl the ball at fearsome speeds. Among the greatest were England's Fred Trueman, Australia's Dennis Lillee, India's Kapil Dev and a number of great West Indian bowlers, including Courtney Walsh, Malcolm Marshall, Andy Roberts and Michael Holding. Among the latest crop of fast bowlers are Australia's Mitchell Johnson and South Africa's Dale Steyn, who was world cricket's 2008 Test Player of the Year.

West Indian fast bowler Courtney Walsh is congratulated by teammates after taking the wicket of England's Mark Ramprakash. Walsh took a total of 519 wickets in Test matches.

Top batting

India's Sachin Tendulkar, Australia's Ricky Ponting and Brian Lara, from the West Indies, have been amongst the best batsmen in the world in recent times. Tendulkar has scored the most Test runs ever (14,240). However, the greatest batsman of all was an Australian who played in the 1930s and 1940s – Sir Donald Bradman. Leading Test batsmen have an average of over 50 runs per innings. Bradman averaged an amazing 99.94 runs per innings.

Donald Bradman with his bat in 1932. Bradman played Test cricket for 20 years (1928–1948) and scored 29 centuries and more than 6,900 runs.

The best team?

Test teams take a number of years to play each other. This makes it hard to judge which side is the best. In recent years, the ICC Test Championship was set up. It is a ranking system based on performances over a four-year period (see page 29). In the past 15 years, Australia have been dominant, but other teams are now competing to be the best.

GREAT SPORTING STATS

Leading Test match run scorers (1877–2010)

Player	Total runs	Average
Sachin Tendulkar (India)	14,240	56.96
Ricky Ponting (Australia)	12,250	56.0
Brian Lara (West Indies)	11,953	52.88
Rahul Dravid (India)	11,602	52.73
Allan Border (Australia)	11,174	50.56

Leading Test match wicket takers (1877–2010)

Muttiah Muralitharan (Sri Lanka)	800
Shane Warne (Australia)	708
Anil Kumble (India)	619
Glenn McGrath (Australia)	563
Courtney Walsh (West Indies)	519

Women's cricket

Women's cricket has a long history. The first women's cricket club was formed in Yorkshire, England, in 1897. The first female Test match was played in 1934 and in 1997 a women's County Championship was set up in England. At international level, teams play Test matches, Twenty20 games, ODIs and a Women's World Cup.

Test matches

There are currently ten teams that play women's Test cricket, with Ireland and the Netherlands joining leading cricket nations such as Australia, England and India in 2000 and 2007 respectively. Matches are mostly held over four days, which has led to many matches ending in a draw – 41 of Australia's 68 Tests have been drawn, for example. Australia and England have so far contested 17 women's Ashes series, with Australia winning six, England four, and seven series drawn.

Australia's opening batswoman, Melissa Bulow, is surrounded by close fielders from India during a Test match.

Limited overs matches

Many women's matches are one-day games, with teams or clubs competing within a country, or one-day internationals with teams playing 50 overs per side. One of the longest running series is the Rose Bowl series between Australia and New Zealand, which has been played every season since 1985. Twenty20 games are also proving popular in women's cricket, with the first Twenty20 World Cup, held in 2009, won by England.

The Women's World Cup

The Women's Cricket World Cup was first held in 1973, and the 2009 competition saw the eight leading women's teams play a total of 25 matches in Australia. England and New Zealand reached the final, where England won the competition for the third time. England's Claire Taylor excelled in the final to become the leading run scorer of the whole tournament.

England's Claire Taylor hits out in the final of the 2009's Women's Twenty20 World Cup. Taylor has scored over 1,000 Test runs and over 3,800 ODI runs for England.

GREAT SPORTING STATS

Australia have the best record in women's ODIs, having won 185 of the 240 games they have played. Their leading player of recent years, Karen Rolton, scored a record 4,814 runs in ODIs and 1,002 Test runs before retiring in 2010.

1877 First Test cricket match between England and Australia.

1889 South Africa plays its first Test match.

1890 First County Championship season in England.

1909 International Cricket Council (ICC) formed.

1932 India becomes the sixth nation to play Test match cricket.

1934 First ever women's Test match is held between England and Australia.

1947 England's Denis Compton scores 3,816 runs, the most in a first-class cricket season.

1948 Australia's Sir Donald Bradman plays his last Test match, against England, before retiring.

1952 Pakistan plays its first Test match against India.

1955: New Zealand records the lowest ever Test match innings, all out for 26.

1968 Sir Garfield Sobers of the West Indies scores six sixes in a single over for the first time in a first-class cricket match.

1973 First Women's World Cup takes place.

1975 West Indies wins the first ever one-day international World Cup, beating Australia in the final.

1982 Sri Lanka becomes the first new Test playing nation in 30 years.

1992 Durham becomes the first new team in the English County Championship for over 70 years.

1994 Brian Lara, batting for Warwickshire, makes the highest ever first-class cricket score of 501 not out.

1997 Highest ever Test match score, 952 runs for 6 by Sri Lanka versus India.

2000 Bangladesh becomes the newest Test playing nation.

2003 First ever Twenty20 competition, the Twenty20 Cup, takes place in England and is won by Surrey.

2005 England win their first Ashes series against Australia since 1986/87.

2007 First ever Twenty20 World Cup held in South Africa and is won by India.

2008 Indian Premier League (IPL) holds its first tournament. Rajasthan Royals win.

2008 India's Sachin Tendulkar passes Brian Lara's world record of 11,953 Test match runs.

2011 Tenth ICC World Cup is hosted by India, Sri Lanka and Bangladesh.

Australia's Donald Bradman (1908–2001) is regarded as the greatest batsman of all time.

Winner tables

ICC Test Championship

Team	Matches	Rating
India	38	129
South Africa	32	116
England	39	112
Australia	37	110
Sri Lanka	27	109
Pakistan	26	88
West Indies	25	85
New Zealand	29	80
Bangladesh	19	7

Cricket World Cup

Year	Winners	Runners-up
1975	West Indies	Australia
1979	West Indies	England
1983	India	West Indies
1987	Australia	England
1992	Pakistan	England
1996	Sri Lanka	Australia
1999	Australia	Pakistan
2003	Australia	India
2007	Australia	Sri Lanka

Twenty20 World Cup

Year	Hosts	Winners	Runners-up
2007	South Africa	India	Pakistan
2009	England	Pakistan	Sri Lanka
2010	West Indies	England	Australia

Women's World Cup Winners

Year	Winners
1973	England
1978	Australia
1982	Australia
1988	Australia
1993	England
1997	Australia
2000	New Zealand
2005	Australia
2009	England

Recent Men's Ashes Winners

Year	Winners
1990–91	Australia
1993	Australia
1994–95	Australia
1997	Australia
1998–99	Australia
2001	Australia
2002–03	Australia
2005	England
2006–07	Australia
2009	England

Glossary and further info

All-rounder A player who is good at batting and either bowling or wicket-keeping.

Bails The small wooden cylinders placed horizontally on top of the stumps.

Batting crease The line running across a cricket pitch 1.22m in front of the stumps.

Boundary The edge of a cricket ground, usually marked by a rope. A struck ball which reaches this rope counts as four or six runs.

Century A score of 100 runs in cricket.

Declare When a team chooses to end their innings before they have lost all their wickets.

Innings The period when a batsman bats until he or she is out and lose their wicket. Can also mean an entire team's turn to bat.

Limited overs Matches where teams each have one batting innings lasting for a set number of overs.

ODI One-day international matches which are either 40 or 50 overs per side.

Over A series of six balls bowled by a bowler from one end of the pitch.

Promoted Moved up a division of a league.

Quarter finals Knockout matches for eight teams with the four winning sides entering the semi finals.

Relegated Dropped down to a lower division of a league.

Round robin A type of competition format where each team plays all the other teams in their group.

Runs Points scored in cricket, most commonly by the batsman hitting the ball and running to the other end of the pitch.

Run-rate The average number of runs scored per over.

Selectors The people who choose the players to form a cricket team.

Semi finals A pair of matches with the winners of each match reaching the final of a competition.

Series A number of events or matches that come one after the other.

Stumps The three wooden sticks placed upright in the ground to form a wicket.

Tailenders Players who bat near the end of an innings who tend not to be known as great batsmen.

Test match The longest and most testing form of cricket, played over five days between two national teams.

The Ashes The name given to the Test match series between Australia and England held every two years.

Twenty20 An exciting new form of cricket in which each team bats for 20 overs.

Wicket A set of three upright sticks with two small sticks on top of them at which a cricket ball is bowled. Also used to describe the area of grass between the two wickets on a cricket pitch, and what a batsman has lost when he is out.

Wicket-keeper The player who stands behind the stumps and fields the ball (should it pass the batsman) using gloves and leg pads.

Websites

http://icc-cricket.yahoo.net
The official website of the International Cricket Council, the organisation that runs world cricket.

http://www.cricinfo.com
An enormous website with fixtures, news, statistics and results on every cricket competition in the world.

http://www.cricket365.com
Another large and comprehensive cricket news website with details of cricket competitions all over the world.

http://www.cricket20.com
A website devoted to all Twenty20 cricket competitions, including details of international games and past and future World Cups.

http://www.ecb.co.uk
The England and Wales Cricket Board's website has lots of information and links to cricket clubs all over the UK, and features on the national men's and women's teams.

http://www.lords.org/latest-news /top-stories
The official website of the cricket ground in London, UK.

http://www.cricket.com.au
The official website of Cricket Australia is packed with features and information on state, national and international cricket.

http://www.caribbeancricket.com
An independent website about cricket competitions in the Caribbean, as well as news and features on the West Indies team.

http://www.blackcaps.co.nz
The official website of New Zealand Cricket, with details of competitions inside New Zealand as well as news of the national team.

http://www.mcg.org.au
The official website of the historic Melbourne Cricket Ground, complete with features and a timeline of major events.

http://www.webbsoc.demon.co.uk
A website full of information on women's cricket, its star players and leading competitions.

http://www.iplt20.com
The official website of the Indian Premier League, with all the latest news about player auctions, matches and leading performances.

Further reading

Young Wisden: A New Fan's Guide to Cricket – Tim De Lisle (A&C Black Publishers Ltd.)
An excellent book about the game of cricket and how it is played.

Inside Sport: Cricket – Clive Gifford (Wayland, 2008)
A guide to the top players, competitions and tactics of cricket.

Index